Manic, Anxious, and the Pursuit of Meds

My Journey

Matthew J. Miller

A somber look into my lifelong battle with bipolar I,
ADHD, generalized anxiety disorder, and PTSD and how
it affected the lives of myself and those around me.

Fulton Books, Inc.
Meadville, PA

Published by Fulton Books 2021

ISBN 978-1-64952-158-3 (paperback)
ISBN 978-1-64952-159-0 (digital)

Printed in the United States of America

CONTENTS

THE TIMES THEY ARE CHANGING

When referencing what is meant to be living through the ever-evolving "new normal" world of COVID-19, Bob Dylan sums it up the best, "The times they are changing."

Panic, anxiety, and fear of the unknown all are thoughts racing through the minds of countless during these times. Many allow anxiety to prompt them in any direction it chooses, plunging them deeper into a cycle of self-loathing.

In my past life, I would have been no different; I would have been physically and emotionally crippled from the onslaught of uncertainty. After my nerves were hijacked, the darkness of depression would soon wrap itself, squeezing every last drop of optimism. Once all remanence of the slightest bit of control seemed futile, I'd feel helpless.

Matt 2.0, the "once was once blind but now can see," keeps his composure and is mindful of what he can and cannot control. I limit opportunities of exposure with others, wears a mask when going out, frequently wash my hands, and practice social distancing to fruition. No longer held back with worry, Matt 2.0 continues to live life to the fullest.

Comparing my mental health to a computer, it wasn't a software problem; it was a hardware problem. My brain needed a complete overhaul to rewire chemical imbalances. Without help, my brain didn't have the tools to fix itself, and I coincidentally struggled to function in society.

I'm not cured but have gone through a 180-degree rewiring following a long overdue treatment plan centered around medication, therapy, and self-care. The aforementioned libation of self-care is for the treatment of my diagnoses of attention deficit hyperactivity disorder (ADHD), bipolar I, generalized anxiety disorder, and post-traumatic stress disorder (PTSD).

More than correcting the chemical imbalances, I have been, in an ever fluctuation of identifying moratorium, never able to establish his own identify. Living my life with the pursuit of happiness, I dithered between different personalities, personas, actions, and beliefs, pursuing whatever allowed me to be as happy as possible. The constant influx never allowed me to settle on a set identity. After piecing together the events of my past, I am better able to understand my present and future.

The following story is inspired by true events. To protect the identity of others, fictitious names and locations are used throughout the story.

ADHD, Anger, and Impulsivity

Growing up with an overabundance of energy, the one constant that provided an outlet of social interaction and a platform to "burn off energy" was organized sports. Often referred to as the "Tasmanian devil kid" growing up, I was a supernova of energy. Pacing back and forth, shaking my legs nonstop, almost incapable of walking, ready to embrace any physical outlet imaginable, I was "that kid."

On the playground, I dominated the horrendously named and highly offensive childhood game referred to as "smear the queer." The object of the game was simple: whoever had the football, you tackled them, pried away the ball, and then tackled whoever had the ball next. In the 1990s, recess was allowed to be much rougher on the playground; such a game would never fly on the playground today.

Regardless of the name, the thrill and joy experienced playing the game motivated me to play as many sports as I could. It wasn't long before I fell for my new love, American football.

Every ounce of anger and frustration, every wiggle and spasm, and every demon I was fighting could be worked out. Like a needle to a vein, I was hooked. I'd show up hours before practice and walk laps around the field waiting for practice to begin. The anticipation made me feel alive, and being part of the team made me feel the sense of belonging I had been searching for. Every time I stepped on the gridiron, I was in transcendence, Nirvana, heaven. My natural success on the field furthered my new obsession.

When I wasn't at the practice or playing in a game, I was dreaming of playing. In the summer months leading to the beginning of the Youth Football League, I would order cleats from the EastBay sports magazine of the 1990s. After the cleats were ordered, I'd have to wait four to six weeks for them to be shipped and delivered. Every day, I'd anticipate waiting for their arrival.

The moment they arrived, I strapped them on my feet and sprinted back and forth in the backyard. Switching the ball to the other arm and giving a stiff arm, I'd fantasize himself scoring the winning touchdown in overtime. In my best Chris Burman voice, I muffled aloud, "He's stumbling…bumbling…could go all the way…!"

The season would arrive, and my mood would follow a predictable high lasting the length of the season. However, after the high of the season had worn off, I'd be hit with the familiar drape of depression. After my team lost the championship game on my sixth grade year, I cried uncontrollably that night and, as I had before, cut myself. Like an Alaskan dreading the day after summer solstice because it officially marks the countdown to winter, football wouldn't return for months later.

That winter, my prediction of doom and gloom didn't occur. Two weeks after football ended, I gave wrestling a try. I had never wanted to try it but was glad I did. Wrestling soon surpassed football as my new passion. Hitting puberty earlier than most of his peers, I was physically bigger and more muscularly developed than similar-aged peers. With brute force and a handful of techniques, I dominated. Wrestling gave him so much esteem, but with the highs of winning came the angst of losing.

When I lost, I felt like a failure in every sense of the word. With all eyes on me, I couldn't hide from failure. If I lost on the mat, I had no one to blame but myself. I couldn't hide among the shadows of a team's loss like I could with football.

I remained undefeated in his sixth-grade year and wouldn't lose a match until the following year. On the bus ride home from the meet, I sat in disbelief as tears fell. I moved several rows ahead, sat next to my coach, and asked him for advice on "what I did wrong." A middle-aged scraggly-looking old man with a thick brown mustache, my's coach, looked at me, shrugged his shoulders in a comforting way, and said, "Stylistically, sometimes, things don't always mesh. It's like that way in life sometimes as well." He continued to comfort me, and after cheering his spirits, he gave me a side hug.

By the eighth grade, I was wrestling varsity. Physically, he could hold his own but still took his share of lumps wrestling opponents up to five years his elder. Although taking my lumps that year, it hardened me up leading him for his athletic career to soar the following year. My head coach was renowned for his ability to get the most out of individuals to push past their limits and achieve their goals.

The year came to an end after an admirable 2-2 record at the sectional qualifying tournament.

My overall baseline of confidence had continued rising, and after, I immediately devoted myself to working out in the gym until the next summer. Reps of 10-8-6 were his go-to. Four times a week, my mother would drop me off at the YMCA so I could work out.

Idealizing the steroid-using character, Steve Lattimer from 1993's *The Program*, I'd pump iron to get as big as he was. I was drawn to his crazy style of play and unleashing his "inner crazy" snarling and grunting like a wildebeest.

The emotions that accompanied my mind turned into fuel for my exercise. I'd read *Flex* and *Muscle & Fitness* magazines getting any top-secret information that would give me that X factor; I did whatever repetitions, sets, and exercises the mags recommended.

Arriving at a football camp at the end of summer for double sessions, I was a solid 170 pounds with abs to match. As a freshman, he made the starting varsity lineup at inside linebacker and went on to have a breakout season. As a linebacker, my job was easy: to follow the flow of plays, cover my assigned gaps, and wrap up when tackling. I would go on to win my team's Most Valuable Player on defense award.

With this newfound acceptance, I was befriended by the older kids that would go on to invite me and give me rides to parties. The objectives at the parties were simple: to get as intoxicated as you could. That's what everyone did so that's what I did. Most times, I would drink until blacking out and vomiting. I'd wake in a friend's house not knowing how I got there.

Seemingly always training or playing, I didn't feel alcohol was affecting my performance, and I could easily "sweat out the booze." By the age of sixteen, I had a fake ID that allowed me the opportunity to purchase my own beer. Many nights, I would drink alone at night if I was feeling stressed or anxious.

It wasn't before long I began driving, while under the influence. Each time I made it home safely, the higher my confidence that nothing bad could ever happen, not to me. Unfortunately, I never was pulled over.

Besides drinking and driving, me and his friends made a game out of reckless driving. One person would do something crazy, and I would feel compelled to top it. Racing friends on the highway at speeds surpassing 120 mph wasn't the only reckless act; on surface streets, I would speed up into the train tracks using them as a ramp to get air.

Unfortunately, my anger boiled over into instances of road rage that were a reactionary catalyst for my use of steroids at seventeen.

With a primary focus on winning and needing anything that would give me the edge, I began taking steroids at the age of seventeen.

I knew what the side effects could be and the dangers, but I didn't care. I wanted to win at any cost. Without hesitation, I began using once making connections to access steroids. I agreed to take whatever the pusher was giving him. It could have rat poison for all I knew, a shot into the side of the ass it would go.

From the lens or the pusher, he saw easy money…an insecure, high school meathead willing to buy whatever was sold.

To afford steroids, I needed money. Steroids weren't cheap; the price per vile was $300. I did whatever I could to feed my addiction. I didn't care who he had to fuck over, steal from, or lie to. Nothing was going to get in my way.

On the field, I dominated but was on a collision course with my inner demons. After my's grandmother passed away my senior year shortly following the end of the wrestling season, my drinking and personal drug use began spiraling out of control.

No longer sticking to just alcohol, I took painkillers to increase his buzz. It wasn't long before beer was substituted with liquor. For countless nights, I'd drive home from parties and not know how he had gotten home. Waking up the next morning to the smell of vomit protruding from the side of my bed, I'd lie physically crippled from the liters of toxic fluid slowly excreting itself through my skin. Natural consequences weren't enough to deter my lifestyle, and I would continue the cycle into college.

Upon moving to college, I was already used to a great deal of freedom as my parents took a laissez-faire approach toward supervision and parenting. Being away from home, the first time wasn't stressful. I continued the same destructive patterns throughout my first semester.

With the excessive levels of drinking, my physical and mental health rapidly decreased. Along with crippling depression, my anger increasingly became violent. With regularity, I got into numerous fights at bars. I couldn't control my anger and was pissed off at the world.

It was only a matter of time before my train derailed. Shortly after returning from winter break, I impulsively pulled a fire alarm walking through campus and was subsequently charged with a felony. Upon being released the next day, I went on a two-day bender that ended after again being arrested for another felony. I jokingly lit a smoke bomb I had procured from the flea market earlier that day and tossed it on his roommate's bed as a prank. I was held in prison for a day and a half before his preliminary hearing. That entire night in the bare white concrete-walled room, all I could think about is how much I wanted to kill myself. Pressing the back of my hand against the damp cold, I felt cold inside and out. Police had taken my shoelaces and belt; otherwise, I would have found a way to kill myself. I thought about taking off my pants and using his jeans as a makeshift noose, but thankfully, the biological need for staying warm was enough to sway my decision.

College Years: Reincarnation and Higher Learning

After being released from jail, I moved back home with my loving parents. That night in the kitchen, my father expressed he was worried about my drinking and didn't want my life to be ruined because of stupid decisions. He didn't yell, he didn't belittle, and he let me know he was there for me and was willing to do anything to help me get better.

To help me stop drinking, my father stopped drinking and made sure there wasn't access to alcohol in the house. Both parents had me attend Alcoholics Anonymous meetings and receive therapy. My mother also pushed him to get back into his previous passion for working out.

My mother was absolutely right: taking his demons out in the gym would absolutely help me kick the booze. When sobering up, I experienced withdrawal symptoms, but they were never too severe for my pain tolerance. My body of nineteen years was able to recuperate with relative ease.

The first few days back in the gym, I could only lift a tenth of what I could before. I'd go through the motions of all the exercises acquired through my own experience and research. I did this extra light workout for about two weeks before strength again began returning.

With my focus on the gym, I still was fighting the hidden demon that dared him to once again use steroids. While living at home, I worked the weekend graveyard shifts at the local McDonald's which allotted me the ability to save my money; once I had enough money, I bought a vile of Sustanon. Sitting in my room, I opened the wrapping of a fresh syringe and paused. I couldn't do it. I knew I didn't want to keep taking the drug so threw it all in the trash. Internally, it was one of the most fulfilling days of my life.

I never opened up to my therapist about my steroid usage, but she still helped me. She had been focusing on building my self-confidence and self-talk. Reluctant at first, the more she applied cognitive behavioral therapy, the better my thoughts became. The better my thoughts, the happier my mood and more positive when viewing myself. Equating to higher levels of self-esteem, I had the strength to kick his steroid addiction for good.

I found support in many of his lifting buddies who themselves were in recovery. After crossing paths at an AA meeting, they shared with me they were living at the local halfway house battling addictions. They pushed me to share my story even though I felt embarrassed. Without the slightest tell of judgment, everyone said, "Thank you for sharing." Everyone allowed me to say what I needed to say, and it felt good.

My mind was anxious about the court case, but after meeting my lawyer, I quickly felt at ease. To ensure my future career as a teacher wasn't compromised, my parents hired one of the best lawyers in the city. After thousands of dollars in fees, all charges of the case were reduced to a year of an adjournment in contemplation of dismissal (ACD). As long as he stayed out of trouble for the next year, I would be in the clear. I was so thankful for all the support given to me every step of the way during those months.

That time in my life was crucial. I reinvented myself like a Rocky Balboa emerging from turmoil to get into the best shape of my life. Physically, I was strong, but more importantly, I was the strongest mentally I had ever been. Instead of working out for the aesthetic value, I focused on getting in the best shape I could. Logically, the better shape he was in, the better my physique would be. This mindset greatly improved my self-esteem. Obsessively working out became the self-medication I needed to battle my depression, anxiety, and ADHD. It would also play a major role in my identities as time progressed.

Transferring to another college that August, I was proud of his progress made with depression and my ability to cope with everyday stressors. I was ready to leave my past behind me and finally move forward. Also, I was ready to get back to competing in sports. Shortly after beginning the next chapter of my collegiate career, I joined the college rugby club.

My ADHD-fueled motor and unusually high pain tolerance made me excel on the pitch. Befriending this new group seemed almost effortless. I could be myself, and there was a true feeling of connectedness. I loved everything about the culture and commodore that came with my new sport.

Willingly, I chose to begin drinking again. However, things were different when I drank. Instead of becoming angry and depressed, I was lively and energetic. Overall, I was happier, and it showed. Physically, my body had more time to recover from hangovers due to my decision to only drink on Thursdays and Saturdays. My "weekend warrior" mentality surprisingly allowed me to find a relatively healthy balance of social life and academics.

As I settled into my new campus, I still hadn't found my self-study skills. Struggling academically adversely translated into elevated levels of anxiety. However, I slowly started improving my academic study skills with self-administered accommodations.

Whenever studying, I'd locate myself as far away from any potential stimuli. The tick of a clock, echoes of footsteps in the distance, slightest change of lighting, sound, or any movement was enough to have me completely lose focus. This "lock yourself in a cave" approach was working. My grades rapidly improved, and the more success I experienced, the more motivated I became to succeed.

My parents were so proud each time I received a 4.0/4.0 GPA. My parents took the grade card and displayed it on the fridge as if I were a schoolboy eager to show his good grades. My parents were right to feel that way; I was so proud of myself.

I finally graduated summa cum laude with highest honors after taking five years to obtain my degree in education. Immediately upon graduating, I began taking classes in pursuit of my master's degree in special education. Attending school full-time, I worked part-time as a substitute teacher until being hired as a paraprofessional at a day treatment school for students with significant emotional and behavioral needs.

During this time, at the age of twenty-four, I began exhibiting early signs of the emergence of bipolar disorder. Almost uncontrollably, I was consumed with negative thoughts and was incapable of filtering the words that came out of my mouth. It was almost as if I would get to know someone just to later turn on them, stopping at nothing to convince others of my thoughts.

Ernest Hemingway describes his earliest experiences with manic depression as becoming "irritable to the point of combativeness" and affected his ability to function in mainstream society. When I was manic, the dark cloud adhered itself in every nook and cranny of his brain. I became ultra focused on the negative in every situation and, for the first time in years, would be consumed with hatred and anger.

I worked with a first-year teacher who had socially been ostracized by those in the building because she attempted to be a whistleblower. When she did, she unintendedly socially isolated herself from the team. To make matters worse, she was a first-year teacher and was struggling. Experiencing the physiological trough of the first year of teaching, she was already in "sink or swim mode."

Instead of attempting to be proactive, collaborate, problem-solve, or just follow directions (without inklings of content), I believed she wasn't good enough for the job. Since she wasn't good enough, she was hurting the team and needed to be fired (for what was best for the group as a whole).

I did everything I could to discredit her. Latching on to the social dynamics of the time, I ran with it. Viewing her already as an outsider to "the team" seemingly fueled my hatred and reinforced patterns of malice thinking. I didn't care if she had children, medical concerns, bills to pay, a mortgage, etc. Unit before self was my motto, and in my mind, I was doing what was best for the team as a whole. I documented anything that could strengthen my argument: she was an inefficient teacher, was bringing down our team, and should ultimately be let go.

The more time at the job, the more my melancholy thoughts overwhelmed the words that blurted out my mouth. I'd speak my truth that, in a dark twisted way, had logic behind it. Colleagues took notice of the negativity that eventually led to me in return being ostracized from the team. When putting in my two-week notice, my principal informed me the proposed grace period was unnecessary and that day would be my last at the organization. I wasn't humbled by my experience and thought nothing of it.

I already had a job lined up as a long-term substitute teacher where I worked until the end of the academic school year. I only had one more semester left until completing my master's degree so he decided to live off my savings while I focused on finishing my program.

That last summer before landing my first teaching gig was my "summer of '69"-like summer. Women, bicycling, working out, and drinking summed up the summer. However, even though the party felt like it would never stop, I was eager to start my career. The problem was in the early 2010s, school districts weren't hiring. They especially weren't hiring teachers with no formal teaching experience. Disappointment soon turned into viewing the situation as an opportunity.

One night, while at his friend's house watching the UFC fight with rugby friends, my friend Nick drunkenly boasted how one day he was going to travel to Montana. When asked why Montana, he'd half-smile and slur his speech saying, "Why the hell not?" Drunk and partially incoherent, he made a good point. If I had the opportunity to travel anywhere I wanted, where would I go? One location that offered such an adventure and was in high need of special education teachers was Alaska.

After applying to numerous jobs on the Alaskan teaching job websites, I received an interview with a K-12 school located in the interior. After a virtual interview that went well, I was hired and had two months to begin planning and say my goodbyes. The time painfully dragged as I couldn't stop perseverating over one thought, the anticipation of moving away for the first time and being on my own. Moreover, I felt I was ready to finally start chipping away at the student loans that had been accruing interest throughout my time in school.

"I've heard it's twenty-four hours of dark. Is that true?" "Bet you'll get a chance to check out the Northern Lights," "I heard…" You get the point. Like a script, every time I exchanged discourse with others revealing I was moving to Alaska, they immediately responded with one of the many questions I had heard hundreds of times prior to my move.

I was nervous as hell but wasn't scared. I had a checklist of everything that needed to be done prior to moving way up north. The first item that needed addressing was gathering needed clothing specifically designed to address subzero temperatures. From bottom to top, I assembled my arctic arsenal consisting of bunny boots (extreme cold vapor barrier boots type II), initial/secondary base layers, bear fleece overalls, and an array of hats, balaclavas, gloves, and a parka. Altogether, the shopping topped $2,000.

After getting the right clothing for Alaska, I bought a one-way ticket to Anchorage that would later be reimbursed by the school district.

Procuring the proper clothing and tickets and making the most out of the time with my support network checked off the list, I had one more task I needed sorting out; for the first time in my life, I was going to buy a car. Blessed, good-fortuned, or whatever one refers to it as, I had always been provided a car by my parents. The hassle of car buying made my head spin. Toyota, Chevrolet, Ford, Hyundai, and the options continued. After carefully examining his options, I settled on buying a new Chevrolet Equinox. This choice seemed to meet my wants and must-haves. To fortify my new chariot into a tank equipped for whatever icy hell Alaska gave, I opted for additional options of studded winter tires, oil pan heater, battery heater, engine block heater, and a nifty attachable cord that plugs into outlets.

Growing up Western New York, I considered myself battle-tested through growing up with occasional bands of lake effect dumping feet of moist snow. Now that I had the gear, ride, and skills needed to make a difference in students' lives, I was ready for my venture. As the time neared, the anticipation heightened with daydreams of how amazing a teacher I was going to be and the once-in-a-lifetime things I was about to experience.

The night before catching my flight up North, I met one last time with friends and family for food and drinks. I returned to my hotel just outside the airport to get as much sleep as I could. With excitement, making sleep next to impossible, I went to the bathroom and looked at myself in the mirror. I knew this was it; I was finally going to make that transition to self-sufficiency and become a man. Nodding my head in agreement to my inner voices, I returned to bed and slowly drifted to sleep.

"Ring, ring, ring...," before the first cycle of alarm clock finished, I was wide-eyed and jazzed ready to begin the day. Jumping out of bed, I turned on the lights, and my eyes did their best to acclimate to the sudden rush of light. Dressing as quickly as I could, I hurried to the airport ensuring Murphy's law wouldn't find a way of me missing my flight. I took the shuttle to the airport, checked my luggage, and located my gate waiting to board the plane. Once locating his gate, I settled in and looked for a place to plug in my laptop. Zipping open my backpack, I spotted a plain white envelope addressed to myself. Immediately, I knew it was from his beloved mother. Opening up the letter, I read it to himself:

Dear Matt,

I never thought this day would come. As bittersweet as it is to see you leave, please know your father and I love you and always will. We are there for you during the best and worst of times. It's hard to see our little boy has grown into a man. Please know we're here for you no matter what.

Love,
Mom

PS. Take some pictures of the aurora borealis.

Eyes stinging with salt and quickly turned bloodshot, my throat fluttered until the tears built up pouring down my face. I didn't care if I looked like a sniveling silly nanny; these words would be the fuel to my fire, the catalyst igniting my passion to change students' lives for the better. Rereading the letter several times, I kissed the letter, put it back in the envelope, and returned it to my bag, keeping a smile painted to his face for the remainder of the day.

An hour passed until boarding began. Both hands clinging to the front straps of his traveling backpack, I presented my ticket and stepped foot on the direct flight to Anchorage, Alaska.

With access to watching television and movies from my seat, the flight passed quickly although I was unable to catch a glimpse of the Alaskan landscape due to the extended hours of darkness. After a smooth landing, I retrieved my luggage from the baggage claim and met up with my new roommate, Mike.

I had spoken to Mike prior to moving on several occasions but had never seen his face (I didn't use Facebook or other social media platforms). Unable to identify my new roommate in the crowd, he called me on his cell phone to locate me. Waving me down by the revolving doors outside the baggage claim, Mike approached with a warm hearty smile and welcomed me to his new world.

Short brown hair, brown eyes, and a stout body reminiscent of the Pillsbury Doughboy, he shook my hand and helped carry my luggage to the taxi procured in front of the airport. We arrived at the hotel as scheduled and ate food at the hotel airport while we chatted. At thirty-three years old, Mike was seven years my elder, but it was also his first year of teaching. He had recently changed careers after spending years as an accountant. Like myself, he had moved to Alaska in search of adventure; specifically, he had moved to Alaska primarily because of his love for hunting and fishing. We conversed and, after a short dinner, decided to call it a night, and each returned to our separate rooms to rest before the following day's journey.

The next morning after waking up disoriented and jet-lagged, I took a taxi to the dealership to pick up my newly purchased vehicle and was then on my way to meet Mike at his house in our town later that evening.

The drive began with breathtaking views of an eerie fogged view of the mountains. However, the temperature continued to drop. Making it through the mountain pass and into the Alaskan Interior, temperatures plummeted to negative thirty degrees Fahrenheit. There was no snow falling from the sky, just an ice-covered road that was unlike anything I had driven in before. Each factor consisting of temperature, humidity, fluctuation of flake size, and crystal structure contributed to driving conditions I had never driven in. After my first two incidents of nearly clipping moose, I slowed down to a comfortable forty-five miles an hour occasionally being passed by semi trucks. Every time I was passed by or passed an oncoming semi truck, a chalky fog would form blinding me for seconds at a time. The four-hour drive quickly ballooned to seven hours.

Not having the ability to receive radio signals and having no music on his phone, the combination of jetlag with fighting the strain of the drive nearly forced me to drift asleep several times along the drive. The true beauty of Alaska was hidden behind a curtain of black laced with skinny coniferous trees on each side. Adding to the dull mental ache, the outdoor temperature had further dropped to negative forty degrees Fahrenheit.

Pulling over on the side of the highway to relieve myself and recharge my energy in the crisp Alaskan air, I looked around me as if every sense was in a whole new world. The crunch of the snow seemed to accentuate the almost complete absence of moisture in the air. Air was crisp to the breath seemingly purified from the extreme cold. With such a barometric detox, conditions were perfect for the absence of any clouds or light pollution permitting viewing every star able to be seen with the naked eye. Such a stop is just what I needed to recuperate and finish the drive.

Arriving drained, Mike met me upon my arrival, helped me with his bags, and directed me to the guest bedroom. Throwing my bags to the corner of the room, I fell face-first onto the portable cot Mike had lent him and fell fast asleep. In lieu of what could be closer compared to a power nap, I woke up and got myself ready for my first day of work.

FIRST DAY OF THE REST OF YOUR LIFE

Reporting to my school building for my first day at work, I was ecstatic to meet my new colleagues. An impromptu welcoming committee greeted me upon entering the building. With no time to waste, I was bombarded by a barrage of questions…

"How was the trip? When did you land? How long have you been in town for?" The clear message repeatedly brought up was that I should have taken a day to rest before coming to work. I could have lost an eye the night before for all he cared, I still would have shown up to work.

After nearly everyone made their introductions and given well wishes, I met my new direct supervisor, Mr. Dan. A tall, gray-haired, clean-shaven charming man had moved to Alaska several years prior to follow his heart and passion for fishing. Like everyone at our school, he was warm and accommodating. However, he stood out from the rest. His charisma made him a natural leader, and it was apparent he was well respected. Whenever he spoke, those around him would listen.

"Matt, how the hell are ya? Welcome!" said Mr. Dan. "Today's going to be a little bit of a blur; we've got allot to go over. I hope you're ready to put on your big boy pants…haha." Leading the way, Mr. Dan gave a tour of the school and facilities with just the two of them. The school wasn't much to explore. In the K-12 school in the Alaskan Bush, each primary grade had a teacher with their own classroom located on the far end of the building. The remaining staff specialized in a subject material and taught numerous grades. For example, his roommate Mike was the math teacher for grades six to twelve.

By the end of the short tour, we arrived in the special education classroom. One large room with approximately seven paraprofessionals that would come and go depending on what student(s) they were assigned to work with. My caseload consisted of an array of differently aged students with a multitude of disabilities. Disabilities consisted of students with one or more of the following: fetal alcohol syndrome (FAS), intellectual delay (ID), autism, specific learning disabilities, Down's syndrome, etc. Out of the twenty-plus students I had on my caseload, nearly half had FAS which occurred with shocking regularity.

Mr. Dan provided modeling and guided practice for the first week prior to handing over the keys to myself. I was in over my head, but I didn't sweat it. As I had done before in college, I was going to plug away and put in the hard work required to get the job done. I wasn't looking for average, "C" grade work; I wanted to give the best "A" quality work I could provide. Grinding away, I showed up early and stayed late spending upward to eleven hours a day at work. I didn't mind the pace or the mental grind; I was giving the job my all and had no regrets. After all, the kids deserved nothing but the best education I could provide.

In the first week of school, I practically lived in my classroom. Just as the first day had come and gone within the blink of an eye, so too did my first week. By the end of the week, I was ready to blow off some steam with some of the other first-year teachers that had invited me to their house for dinner and drinks. I had been so immersed in my work I hadn't even thought about allowing myself to have fun.

On that Friday, the dinner party was hosted by the music teacher Chris and his friend Josh (who was substitute teaching for the school). I was ready to "party it up" as Chris and Josh openly gloated. The evening began with food, music, drinks, and conversation. As evening transitioned to night, the "older crowd" filtered out one by one leaving the younger staff to kick their drinking up a notch.

I felt like I was back in New York with drinking buddies I had known for years; I was eager to bond over bottles with my newly made friends. Unfortunately, my drinking was "kicked up a notch" but not in a way that garnished positive attention. After numerous drinking games, I blacked out and didn't remember anything from the night. Apparently, the group went to the local bar for a night of karaoke. Bumbling and slurring my speech, I gave his best rendition of George Michaels "Careless Whisper." The rest of the night, I was my usual flamboyant self when drunk.

Being a small town, everyone knew of my business and my night of drinking. Later that week, I stopped by the administration building to complete some paperwork. When walking through the doors, the receptionists smiled and began applauding jokingly requesting an encore of my choice of karaoke. Although they weren't overly judgmental, there's no telling what others may have thought about me. I didn't seem too worried about the ordeal and brushed it off as "hazing the rookie" and just "having fun."

Friday was merely the tip of the iceberg when letting out steam and decompressing. My favorite activity that was one of the main factors that swayed my decision to move to Alaska was my passion for hiking and exploring nature. Waiting until Sunday for my hangover to subside, I met with my newly made friend from Friday's party, Alex.

A frumpy man in his early thirties always wore his favorite pair of wool overalls and pair of bunny boots with laces knotted to transform his boots into what he referred to as "Alaskan slippers." His five o'clock shadow complemented his ruffled, hat hair that was left short. Despite his unkempt appearance, he'd light a room with his patented smile that displayed both rows of his plaque stained teeth. He worked as a local EMS worker, and his wife taught in the district as an elementary school teacher. Like Max, Alex was impulsive and full of energy which he attributed to his ADHD. We were like two peas in a pod. More specifically, we both embraced the lifestyle of "you only live once so you better make it count."

The first hike was epic. Sharing a backpack full of snacks and cans of Hamm's, we strapped on snowshoes and hiked the best we could through the conditions. Following an old logging road whose incline continued to rise with no end in sight. Every half a mile or so, we would take a beer break. After drinking a beer, we'd return to our hike. After we were plenty drunk and had to pee every other minute, Alex recommended we use the cans as target practice. I had never fired a gun before and was on my Alaskan bucket list. Using Alex's 30-aught-six rifle, I placed the butt of the gun to the front of my left shoulder, steadied the barrel with my adjacent hand, and did my best to aim. The first shot sent a jolt through my body instantly releasing a rush of energy. "PSHEEEEEEEEEEWWWWWWWWWW" echoed throughout the trees as nearby ptarmigans fled the area. After my first shot, I exhaled a deep sigh of relief and with wide-eyed excitement proclaimed with a gleam, "That was fuckin' awesome! How have I never done this before?" After a dozen attempts, I finally heard the ting of hitting one of the beer cans.

With Alex by his side, I purchased my first handgun later that week. A .44 short-barreled Magnum with plenty of stopping power to give me a fighting chance if ever in the position to defend myself from Alaskan wildlife. With ammo being close to a dollar a bullet, I also bought a .22 pistol for when I was doing target practice. Expensive but well worth the buy to give a new sense of security.

Our friendship grew the more time we spent with one another. Hiking, working out, drinking, and shooting guns became our go-to entertainment activities. The more sunlight to work with, the more adventures we had. However, not everyone was as thrilled we had formed such a close bond.

Alex was married, and his wife was not too keen on me. She'd nag Alex not to hang out with me so much because "we'd end up in jail" because of the way we acted when they were together. She also became jealous of the amounts of time Alex was away from home fraternizing and felt her emotional needs were not being met. Alex continued hanging out with me, but our time spent with one another became less frequent as time continued.

Bummed that I didn't have the opportunity to hang out with Alex more often, I continued my hobbies solo. It wasn't the same. Everything in the outside world was beautiful, but I couldn't match the feelings I had when my friend was with me. I became down, but not depressed. I still had his job as a special educator which gave me the intrinsic gratification I sought. Everything appeared to be going well at my job. I was making leaps and bounds from my initial baseline and held a good working relationship with my colleagues and supervisor, Mr. Dan.

Although change can be good, Mr. Dan's demeanor also changed during this time. Always appearing genuine and trustworthy, his persona one day suddenly shifted. In a 180-degree switch of moral intentions, he became irate at the paraprofessional, Rhianna, and showed a side of himself that hadn't been shown before. After showing up a few minutes late to a professional development (PD) session that was being presented by Mr. Dan, he reprimanded her in front of her peers and informed Rhianna (in front of her peers) since she had shown up late, she should leave and would not be getting paid for the day. I thought this was way too much but didn't want to get in the middle of others' affairs. Besides, I seemed to be on the "good side" of politics. Shortly after, she filed a grievance to the Union claiming she had been publicly shamed and humiliated. She was right; she had been.

The next day, while conversing with Mr. Dan in his office behind closed doors, he openly spoke how he felt he had been "told on." He was in dismay he could have done something wrong and felt as if he was the victim and she was in the wrong. Candidly leaning back on his chair, he put his hands behind his head and calmly said, "Well…Rhianna won't be coming back next year, not after pulling that shit." After adding a few insults at Rhianna's integrity and character, he proceeded to tell me he was going to make sure her life was made miserable in any way he could. As he phrased, she would be "shaking in her boots."

Instructed to build ammo to build a case for termination, I was directed to follow her, documenting anything that could be used against her. Specifically, I was to round down to the nearest minute whenever she arrived or left a classroom. Any word, gesture, or mannerism displayed that could be skewed into something more was documented. Seeking the approval of Mr. Dan, I followed orders without hesitation.

The time following the incident, Mr. Dan openly made disparaging comments about Rhianna in front of myself and his colleagues. Although I didn't agree with what was going on, I wanted to stay on Mr. Dan's good side. I figured it was better such treatment be happening to someone else than myself.

A greater level of social alienation accompanied Rhianna moving forward. She felt hopeless about the situation and did her best to solely focus on her job and ignore gossip. She had a feeling she was being targeted as a form of retaliatory actions but had no way of proving it.

That spring break, the all too familiar cycle of depression took over. Most of my acquaintances had left town for the break, and I was on my own to entertain myself. Colors lost their brightness, optimism lost all hope, and my world reverted to the doom and gloom I had struggled with for much of his life. I didn't understand; this is what I wanted. I was getting paid a competitive salary, had insurance, and could make payments toward my student loans; how could I not be happy?

Upon returning, I still wasn't my usual self but couldn't wait to get back into the classroom. Teaching gave me a purpose in life and allotted me the ability to directly help students and make a difference in their lives. Nothing else mattered as long as I still had the opportunity to follow my passion.

Days after returning from spring break, I was called down to the office for a meeting with Mr. Dan and the superintendent. Contracts were being handed out for the proceeding academic school year, and I thought it was my turn to receive mine. I could tell something was off about Mr. Dan. His usual warm self was reserved, and he only spoke a few words. The superintendent began the meeting saying, "I want to make this quick. There's no easy way of saying this, but unfortunately, your contract will not be renewed for the following school year."

Absolutely blindsided, I pleaded for a reason as to why I wouldn't be returning. I didn't understand; I had given my all and would do anything for my students. I was passionate about making a change and was motivated by the right reasons. No reason was provided other than the job "wasn't a good fit."

Naive my drinking and lifestyle portrayed me as an alcoholic, I couldn't accept that I hung my own professional noose. Through gossip, the entire community knew of my personal business and rambunctiousness. Although I fancied myself the "life of the party," the reality was in the world of teaching, the public's view can make or break an individual. Seemingly under a microscope of the public's eye, every action became public knowledge. Making the decision to part ways was politically best for the district.

Once the bombshell dropped, I had the wind completely zapped from his lungs. My mind wouldn't allow me to move forward. I couldn't... What went wrong? What had I done? Could this have been a big misunderstanding? Not being given a reason as to why I was nonrenewed, I quickly felt betrayed by Mr. Dan. I had been recruited to pack up and move away for the first time thousands of miles away from my support network. I left my old life behind me and wanted the next chapter in life to take place in Alaska. With so many emotions swirling in my mind, panic, and fear quickly set in.

Along with becoming suspicious, I became weary of Mike who was fishing buddies with Mr. Dan. With both being so close, I assumed Mike had known about this and was in on it. With his mental health spiraling, I had one area of concern that had haunted me for years, the boulder of debt whose interest had accumulated over seven years. Anxiety and paranoia got the best of me, and I rationalized I needed to save money in order to better preserve my financial future. However, this meant moving out of my current living situation and living out of my car until I figured something out. Mike hadn't done anything wrong to me, but in a drama-filled evening, I abruptly packed up my belongings and moved them into my car.

With two months until the end of the school year, I easily could have afforded to pay for an extended stay at one of the local hotels. Although much of my paycheck would be spent, I would be paying for basic needs such as warmth and a sense of security.

I could have quit, accepted this as a setback in my career, and drove back to his parents' home until getting back on my feet. My loving parents would welcome me back with open arms and help me get back on my feet just as they had done when he was kicked out of college following my arrests. I would have had a warm bed, plenty of food, and the ability to save money.

Neither were options I wanted to entertain. The shame and guilt of being twenty-six years old and being informed I was not wanted back were almost unbearable. Even if I returned home, it made me feel like less of a man that he couldn't support himself. At twenty-six years old, I still couldn't take care of myself. That's what hurt the most.

I made a decision based on what would save me the most money and what would allow me to keep my pride; I chose to live out of my car for the remaining time left on my contract. The less money spent, the more money I'd have. The more money, the greater sense of financial security, the overall happier I'd be in the months following my crash and burn professional genesis. At least, this was the logic of a manic self who was almost completely out of touch with reality.

My father pleaded to pay for a hotel room for me or, at the least, accept money sent my way. Each offer was refused based on pride. Some may consider my actions noble, but most would consider such a decision foolish. My logic held true, but the value of safety and security were significantly undervalued. Over the span of the next two months, my body along with my sanity deteriorated.

My first night of "car camping," I knew the perfect place that only someone that had flown over the cuckoo's nest would decide to settle in and refer to as his new home. I parked in the graveyard and used the location as my "go-to" nighttime sleep spot. Being April, outdoor temperatures dropped to ten degrees Fahrenheit. I used wool blankets that first week to attempt to keep warm.

Sprawled out in the back of my SUV with the seats folded down, the cold quickly overcame my car as ice formed a thick layer of crystals on the inside of the windows. Unable to fight the urge to fall asleep, I drifted only to be woken by the chattering of my teeth. I would turn the car on allowing heat to fill the car and turn the car off once warm enough. Turning off the car, I'd sleep in quartered shifts until I again woke up shivering and repeated the cycle.

The first several weeks were hell on his body. my body ate away at his fat reserves as it did its best to maintain body heat; combining this with a loss of appetite, my weight quickly plummeted to unhealthy levels. More than the physical challenge of sleeping through frigid conditions, my mind was becoming completely unhinged.

My mind already consumed with a whirligig of demons, I contemplated suicide numerous times. One night after feeling I no longer could keep fighting, I wrapped my mouth around the barrel of my .44 Magnum. As tears fell in lieu of devastating internal shame, I felt I didn't deserve to live anymore. I was a child in a man's body, unable to cross the bridge into adulthood. My teeth began chattering around the metal of the barrel, and I pictured how quick and painless it would be to throw in the towel.

With music already playing in the background from the XM radio, Young the Giant's song, *Cough Syrup*, began playing "Life's too short to even care at all… Oh…I'm losing my mind, losing my mind, losing control…" As if a divine intervention of fate saying it wasn't my time, I opened his eyes and removed the gun from my mouth. I had wanted to die, but the song lifted my spirts just enough to keep giving my life a try.

On the verge of suicide, there was another passion that lifted me from the depths of despair, travel. Previously looking for emotional support, I spoke to my colleague Kate who advised me to take full advantage of the abundance of nature Alaska had to offer. She was right; this is just what I needed, something to look forward to.

Knowing I was the "dead man walking" at work, I stopped caring about the job and gave little to no effort. Self-reflecting, I felt I had already been fucked over and realized it wasn't worth offing himself over a job. Checking out did wonders for my mental health. "Fuck 'em," I told myself. I was going to explore as much of the state as he could with the little bit of time I had left. After all, I had unused personal days and sick time waiting to be used up. These mini vacations proved to be chicken noodle soup for my soul. Traveling all across the state, I visited wherever the system of highways would take him.

During my first trip, I took a four-day weekend vacation driving to Homer located on the Kenai Peninsula. Unlike my first long drive in Alaska, driving conditions were much more accommodating, and I had plenty of sunlight to work with. Arriving in Homer, every image looked as if it could be a cover photo of an Alaskan calendar. Exhausted from my drive, I found the nearest bar and drank a pitcher beer from the Alaskan Brewing Company. Sitting in the bar, I felt so relieved I could be out in public and be left alone. I hadn't felt a sense of anonymity in months, and it felt good. I felt he could be myself. Retreating to my car for the night, I planned a hike for the next day before resting and heading back to my town on Monday.

The following week, I again planned a trip, but this time, I was bound for Valdez. The previous weekend had made me feel alive again. I felt I could be mindful of the world around him and wholeheartedly appreciated all nature had to offer. Beyond the scope of hiking trails, I climbed as high vertically as I could on the face of the mountains easily accessed from the side of the highway. Dismissing avalanche risk, I strapped on my snowshoes and vertically hiked as high as my body could muster for the day. Just as I would when hiking, I would take beer breaks. Casually sitting in the snow and wiggling my body, I would mold my own little "snow couch" and settle in. For the first time in his life, I felt I truly understood what it meant to be mindful of the world around him. The chill of the wind howling from every direction, contrasts of whites and darks, smooth to rough surfaces, and snow to rock...all took my breath away.

The last trip consisted of me enjoying the big city conveniences of Anchorage and exploring the hiking trails around the Mat-Su Valley. My return to "civilization" made me long for my contract to be up so I could "hit the reset button" and move forward.

With two weeks left in the academic school year, the paraprofessional Rhiana extended the offer for me to stay at her house in their spare bedroom until I was ready to go home. In a warming, soft voice, she said, "Come and go as you please... You're always welcome here."

Although opening her home to an individual was the moral and ethically right thing to do, she still had a hidden agenda. She knew she had been targeted by Mr. Dan after going to the Union and wanted to get him back. She wanted me to be aware of what was going on regarding said words and actions directed at myself. Just as Mr. Dan had fixated all his anger toward Rhianna making her life hell, she communicated she had observed the same hatred and mal-treatment directed toward myself. She wasn't stretching the truth; she was stating observations.

After I abruptly moved out of my rented house, Mike was gypped out of half his monthly rent each month which greatly upset him. It wasn't long before Mike and Mr. Dan's personal bond cor-related into retaliatory actions.

Through hearsay, Rhianna informed me there seemed to be a shift in who Mr. Dan focused all his energy on when upset. She described at the moment, I was the "flavor of the week." Mr. Dan would openly talk about me despairingly in front of my colleagues and paraprofessionals. Also, shared through hearsay he was trying to get me fired before my contract was up. Although I hadn't done any-thing wrong, I was angry and for good reason. Believing such dirty politics needed to be exposed, I composed a grievance detailing the unethical political makeup of the school (specifically the actions of Mr. Dan) I felt created a hostile environment.

So proud of myself for doing the right thing, I was on cloud nine. The feeling wouldn't last.

Two days after filing the grievance, a meeting was held with the superintendent, Mr. Dan, and myself; I should have had a Union representative but chose not to have one. With the two side-by-side across the table, the superintendent began the meeting saying, "So, I heard you hit a student over the head with a book." Mr. Dan quietly breathed out his nose and released a quick, subtle chuckle.

Jaw-dropping to the floor such words would be uttered, I was falsely accused of forcefully hitting a student over the head with a book.

I rebutted this as true only to be responded with, "That's not what I heard." I immediately advocated for myself saying this was untrue and questioned why my grievance had fallen on deaf ears. Not even entertaining the question, the superintendent conveniently slid into the presentation of what he referred to as a "one-time deal."

I was told I needed to agree to and sign administrative leave papers or "the deal was off." The meeting was Friday after school, and I was given until Monday morning to give them an answer.

That weekend, I had had enough of my ordeal, I just wanted to leave and go home. Ready to get the hell out of Dodge, I signed the papers as soon as I could Monday and was immediately off on a multiple-day voyage spanning thousands of miles.

My mind and soul became hypermanic, giving me the energy of averaging 1,000 miles of a day before crashing and taking a rest. I couldn't help it. Flight was the only response he knew. With trauma stoking the coals of mania, he couldn't account for much of the drive due to "highway hypnosis" and drove much of the trip with his never-ending thousand-yard stare.

Shortly after crossing the Canada-US border into Montana, I received a call from my sister in Missouri. She had been attempting to contact me, but I had turned off my phone while driving through Canada. Finally reaching me, she reassured me everything was going to be okay, and said, "Fuck em…come stay with us until you figure out your next step." When I needed family the most, family stepped up. Instead of trekking back to New York, I stopped and spent the next few weeks in Missouri with the plan of "getting things sorted out".

When reaching his sister's house, I immediately broke down and began hysterically weeping. Like a blister being oozed of its puss, my body needed to release the emotions I was feeling. Over the span of the next two days, I continued crying until eventually falling asleep. Sleeping for the day and a half, I only left the guest bedroom a few times to go to the bathroom and then immediately returned to bed. Every ounce of his body was drained, but my spirits quickly rose realizing once again that my past was behind me.

REST, RELAXATION, AND
THE LOVE OF HIS LIFE

Staying with my sister provided the support I needed to decompress. While my sister was at work, I coped the way I had always before. I worked out nonstop from the second I woke up to the second my sister arrived home from work. Taking advantage of the Midwestern heat, I swam for hours while at the same time drinking heavily. By late morning, I had already achieved my sought after "first buzz of the day." My buzz only intensified the more booze I poured into my system; at times, I would go through a bottle of liquor in a day's time.

The trifecta of sunshine, exercise, and alcohol seemed like just what the doctor had ordered. It was enough to get me out of my "funk," and my mood once again improved. However, mentally, I wasn't in the clear. Any sight, sound, or touch that reminded me of Alaska brought with me uncontrollable anxiety. I tried but couldn't shake the ordeal out of my head. To further cope, I blacked out as much of my experience I could. I cut off all ties to anyone I knew in Alaska and wanted everything about the experience to be a thing of the past.

I was able to recompose myself and continued applying for jobs around the country. After a short two weeks, I was interviewed and hired for a high school special education position in the urban core of Kansas City. Still shaking the jitters of my first full-time work experience, I remained optimistic this was my second chance that wasn't going to be squandered. Giving myself plenty of time to adapt to my new city, I moved into an apartment downtown.

Settled into my new environment, I optimistically began my new job. The first day provided the typical mandatory all-staff meeting. Gathered in a circle, the staff took turns in clockwise order introducing themselves and providing a fun fact about themselves.

Across the room on the opposite end of the circle, I caught a glimpse of my future everything, Juneall. Tall, thin, and beautiful, she was the most physically attractive woman I had ever laid eyes on. Her natural hair permed straight and lightened by the summer sun accentuated her caramel skin that radiated gorgeousness. Besides her physical traits, she appeared to have a reserved, shy personality that added to a sense of mystery.

I hoped I would be partnered up with her for one of the activities but wasn't so fortunate. I would have to wait till later in the afternoon for my chance to get to know her. Intimidated, I knocked on her door and introduced myself. Greeted with a warm smile, she welcomed me into her office.

Juneall had recently moved to Kansas City after graduating with her undergraduate degree in social work. She was hired as the social worker/"community liaison" for the school. Like myself, she loved helping others and wanted to make a career out of it. Through small talk, we got on the topic of what each other has been doing for fun since moving to Kansas City. I responded with a grin, "That's a good question… What do I do for fun? I know… I like hanging out with you and meeting up sometime after work to grab a drink." As clumsy as I could be around women, I was pretty smooth that day. It worked, and we made plans to get drinks the following day after work.

We met at a college bar on the east side of town for $2 pitchers of domestic beer. It wasn't the cleanest, and the décor could easily be considered as tacky, but their prices were the best in town. Sitting on weathered stools held together by duct tape, we continued our discussion from the day prior to conversing likes and interests. Volleying questions back and forth, we enjoyed each other's company while we sipped our beer. After the best two hours of my life, we called it a night and returned to our separate apartments.

At the time I was online dating and had already made arrangements to go on a date with a different woman that Friday. During the entire date, I couldn't stop thinking about Juneall. I hurried along with the date as quickly as it could so afterward he could see if Juneall was free and available. After parting ways with my date, I immediately called Juneall, and we met to get her favorite food, pizza. Continuing our enchantment for one another, we further conversed and decided to get drinks after.

At that time, I was in a phase of stealing pint glasses from bars to "add to my collection." After leaving the bar, I looked over at my angel and grinningly said, "I got this for you… Consider it a souvenir." She laughed and unzipped her purse. After fumbling around with the zipper for a bit, she pulled out a pint glass she too had taken from the same bar! Without hesitation, I leaned in, and we shared our last "first kiss" of their lives. After, we continued walking holding hands as we joked we were "partners in crime" like Bonnie and Clyde.

After that weekend, we did every kind of date you could imagine: biking, hiking, dancing, painting, movies, dinners, etc. Especially at the beginning of their relationship, we were young and only wanted to enjoy each other's company and have a good time. It didn't matter if we only had $10 between them; we still found ways of having fun. As the fun continued, our relationship continued to grow; more than a physical connection, we connected on a deeper emotional level.

After the trough of a manic low experienced less than a year prior, my happiness plateaued and perfectly synced with the beginnings of our love. Inseparable does not begin to describe what we were to each other. We fell for each other hard. After dating for only six months, we decided to move in together.

Plato quotes, "True love is admiration." We weren't identical, but as we grew, so too did our complimentary virtues making each other our better half.

Together, we had so much fun that year—young and in love while making the most out of every day. My emotional needs were being met allowing me the ability to not stress (as much) and freak out about the stressors of my job. I learned the nuances of the job and continued making progress. I had support from my principal and was receiving positive feedback. I had an excellent group of students along with an experienced paraprofessional who was amazing at doing her job. I was set up for success and was making the most of my opportunity.

The year flew, and I felt like my old self again. Confidence soaring, I was offered a higher paying teaching job for the suburban districts I referred to as "The Big Leagues" of teaching. With stellar recommendations from my year of excellence, I was "snatched up" by the neighboring suburban school that immediately boosted my income by over $10,000. Finally, it was the opportunity of a lifetime, and all the years invested in my education were finally paying off.

Summer came and went, merely an extension of good times that seemed would never end. However, good times did more than end; they came to a crashing halt. In my mind, I thought emotionally, I was in the clear from the fallout of my first teaching experience. After a week of beginning my new job, it quickly became apparent I was in over my head. Only being able to compare it to short-circuiting, my body went haywire, and I continued having nightmares of again losing my job and being homeless. With severe anxiety and fear, I couldn't eat, sleep, or think about anything other than worrying he was going to lose my job.

By October, I had been placed on a performance improvement plan (PIP) and been told if my work didn't improve at the appro-priate rate, my contract would be nonrenewed. Already in panic mode and fighting a cocktail of untreated conditions, the extra stress became toxic. I chipped away at the professional workings of the job the best to my ability and made substantial progress. However, like a red dot on my forehead, my principal had already made her decision I wouldn't be coming back.

Every time the principal did a formal or informal observation, she omitted any and all positive comments, only leaving the negative. To me, I knew what was happening; she was compiling documen-tation to justify my nonrenewal, the "writing was on the wall" and "my time was up," a week before the latest possible date to distribute contracts for the following school year.

For months, I clung on to hope everything was all in my head and I would receive my contract for the next school year. Finally, the week before the deadline for contracts being administered, I asked her if I was getting a contract for the following year. Allowing me the opportunity to leave on my own terms, she carefully phrased her words saying, "Right now, I don't know… I'd say there's a fifty-percent chance." I could leave my Alaskan experience off my resume, but being nonrenewed inevitably would nearly destroy my career (as nonrenewed teachers are often blacklisted from future schools). I chose to resign shortly after avoiding the potential of being nonrenewed.

Once I officially informed my job I was choosing to resign upon completing my contract, a wave of tension that had been eating away at me for months took over, and just as in Alaska, I stopped caring and made plans to travel. I knew I didn't have any favorable references so I half-assed the job. The principal had shown how she had felt toward me, and in return, I had no motive to "put on my happy face." With spring break approaching that weekend, Juneall talked me into taking a road trip to Colorado.

The mountains were just what I needed to again live life and for a brief point, forget about everything that had gone wrong in the past few years. Renting a cabin in Vail, we enjoyed a winter wonderland and chose to "celebrate life." Just as flashbacks visited me from time to time, the good memories tied to travel all returned as well as lifting my spirits and brightening my mood. We had such a memorable experience; Juneall traces the beginnings of her love of travel to this trip.

Upon returning, I connected with some of his contacts at his most previous job in the urban core and found a job working in one of the district's middle schools. Unfortunately, the job was available because teachers frequently quit from the school environment. I knew it would be tough but was confident I could take students' worse.

Unrenowned to myself, I had PTSD and ADHD; loud noises were one of my major triggers. Painting the picture of how the school year went, students would run figure eights up and down the hallway screaming at the top of their lungs. Along with the auditory flare-ups, fights would spontaneously erupt only to be broken up with security pepper spraying the students to make them disperse. With all the stimuli bombarding my brain, I lost his cool on several occasions resulting in me screaming at students and staff alike. I couldn't control it, I didn't know what was wrong with me, but whatever it was, I couldn't keep it bottled inside.

That March, for the third time in four years, I was informed I wouldn't be returning the next academic school year. That summer, following the pledge to Juneall to be checked by a professional regarding my mental health, I saw a primary physician believing it would meet the criteria of seeking the appropriate level of professional help. I knew something was wrong but continued downplaying the severity of my experiences.

He scheduled an appointment to see my primary physician for what I thought was merely anxiety. Desperate to open up, I described my symptoms the best I could and briefly described some of my experiences which slowly painted a picture of trauma. Quickly recommending I ought to seek help in the form of counseling, she attempted to persuade me into accepting therapy would be beneficial. Growing up with a "chiseled from granite" mentality, I believed men don't do therapy and such endeavors would make him less of a man. Choosing not to receive help proved foolish in years' time but, nonetheless, was a decision I wasn't ready to commit to. Moreover, I refused to take the beginning dosage of Zoloft prescribed. Counselors and therapists reached out numerous times over the next year offering assistance, but I remained stubborn.

HOW MANY CHANCES
DO YOU NEED?

Embarrassed and ashamed, I felt like a complete failure. I was twenty-eight, had a master's degree, and couldn't hold down a job. I applied to numerous districts but didn't receive any calls. Knowing options were limited because of my choppy work past, I applied to a day treatment school that catered to the emotional and behavioral needs of students. The school had an average teacher shelf life of a year which I figured sounded about right given the environment that accompanies similar schools. Hesitant, but knowing I didn't have any other options, I accepted the job offer when given and enjoyed the rest of Summer.

After securing another teaching gig, I celebrated the best way me and Juneall knew how, we took a road trip up north to Quebec City. Not quite ready for the nerves that accompany boarding a plane and traveling across the world, Quebec City was perfect for her comfort level. Most people spoke English and the culture, although more akin to French, was similar to America. That trip, they explored the city on bicycles. My favorite memory was biking below the Fairmont Le Château Frontenac and making day trips scaling the paths along the St. Lawrence River. The trip was just what we needed to enjoy our Summer.

Once August arrived, I knew his vacation was over. I didn't quite know what awaited me at the day treatment school, but if it were anything like my first experience in such a setting when I was a paraprofessional, I knew he was in for a rough go.

Unlike when he was a paraprofessional in a 6:1:1 classroom setting, staff to student ratio was 12:1:1. This made for "sticky situations." Worse, I was still developing as an educator and didn't yet have the skills to provide an emotionally safe environment. This quickly gave way to students increasingly being in crisis and a corresponding spike in restraints. I was struggling and didn't know how or why.

Until around Thanksgiving, the class was bonkers. Students flying into crisis all hours of the day, I would have up to five restraints in a day's time: screaming, punching, kicking, calling you every obscenity imaginable, threatening false accusations, having bodily fluids thrown at you, and going AWOL, you name it. I figured out why the school had the reputation it did… It was exhausting. A person can only take an overexposure to such vicarious trauma for so long before both their physical health and mental health begin to deteriorate.

I didn't understand why the hell students' behavior wasn't getting better; it was getting worse as the year continued. He cared for every student and was doing his best to provide a safe environment and be "trauma sensitive." Observing the more established staff, I noticed a common theme: kindness was weakness. Being Mr. Nice Guy wasn't working at all.

Watching a re-run of *Full House*, my philosophy toward behavior changed after watching the episode; it seemed to speak to my situation. In the episode, the fun-loving jokester, Uncle Joey, was bestowed the job of "babysitting" his teenage nieces who subsequently walked all over him. When he attempted to confront them about the actions, he wasn't taken seriously and subsequently blatantly disrespected.

The message in his mind was clear: he needed to put his foot down and no longer play the role of "cool uncle" or the "nice guy." The next day, I completely shifted my demeanor, tone, pitch, facial expressions…anything I could to ensure I wasn't perceived as "Mr. Nice Guy." Just as an actor stays in character, I adopted the mentality until behaviors were put in check. Restraints drastically decreased in numbers as the year progressed.

With newfound examples of success, I again discovered my passion for teaching that had appeared to be long gone and forgotten. The more time I spent in the meat grinder, the more I observed what approaches and techniques do and do not work for certain students.

I did whatever was effective at stunting behaviors before they could escalate. Morals and ethics became an "open to interpretation" grey area where at times, I was thrown into situations where he would have to choose between the "lesser of two evils."

Adapting as the year progressed, I produced results that impressed many of my colleagues. Through trial and error, I made progress. Although I was "knocking it out of the park," there was still an area of contention in the back of my mind; contract renewals. Every day, I was in a constant state of hyperarousal, fearing the inevitable was bound to happen. It was not a matter of if I would lose my job but, more appropriately, when would I lose his job.

One morning, my supervisor called me into her office. Anytime I interacted with her, I'd get choked up, bumble my words, and struggle not to allow my body to shake. I didn't know why my anxiety would elevate any time I went near her. "Right to the point," she said, "well, Mr. Matt, we are pleased to offer your contract for next year if you would give us the honor of returning." Like a kid drooling over his crush, I couldn't say anything; I tried, but the words wouldn't come out. After a brief period of awkward silence, I smiled, agreed, and signed my contract.

Finally! I was coming back for another year! I was ecstatic to tell Juneall the news. She was so happy for me claiming she hadn't seen me this happy in years. For another year, I had job security lined up. It didn't matter most days I was deprived the opportunity to take the smallest of breaks including planning time and a duty-free lunch, I had loyalty to the school that was willing to give him the shot I had floundered so many times before.

With the confidence of landing my first contract renewal in several years, I began saving money for our next trip which brought us to Ireland the following winter.

Juneall and I were ready for our first trip abroad. I had been in contact with Connor, a high school friend that was an Irish exchange student. We had kept in contact but never figured I would have the opportunity to visit. Arriving on St. Steven's day (the day after Christmas), we hopped a taxi and were dropped off at Connor's house. Same build, same face, with a lot less hair on his head… He was the same Connor. Eager to paint the town emerald green, we all began "pregaming" for the night's festivities as soon as we arrived. Surprisingly, Connor and the majority of his friends drank American domestics; particularly, they loved Coors Light served over ice.

That night, we attended one of the city's pubs that was hosting live music. In a swirl of drunken euphoria, me, Juneall, Connor, and acquaintances pounded our pint glasses on our bar table to the beat of the drums and would later dance. Eager to welcome the Americans to Dublin, numerous free drinks were passed our way. "Painting the town emerald green," we drank and partied harder than we had ever before. Exploring the city on foot, we stopped by every pub along the way and had a drink as if it were commonplace to randomly stop every few minutes and "pop in to have a pint."

I never had time to physically recover and vomited more than I cared to admit. We finally visited St. James' Gate (Guinness Brewery) to take the tour. After, we had the opportunity to pour our own pints of Guinness. I had been looking forward to "tasting the freshest sip of Guinness I had ever had." Throughout the tour, I continuously dry heaved, and my heart felt like it was palpitating. When I had the opportunity to experience the "best Guinness of my life," I couldn't do it. The mere smell of anything with a hint of alcohol sent me running for a garbage can.

After the trip, Juneall and I were hooked on international travel. She said she had never felt so alive in her life. Being a woman of color, she joked she was Black and Irish because she loves the music, food, beer, and people so much that she's an honorary Irishwoman. St Patrick's Day continues to be her favorite holiday even though her parents (who are both African American) jokingly yell at her, "You're not Irish!"

After the trip, I was feeling different toward my relationship with Juneall. Even before the trip, I had been thinking about asking Juneall to marry me but was nervous. I knew we loved each other but didn't know if she was ready to take the next step. Reflecting on the plane ride from Dublin, I thought of all the examples of unconditional love I had observed. My grandma and grandpa were the prime example of "till death do us part"; they were married for sixty-five years before my grandpa passed away of natural causes. I thought of the love his parents had for one another, being married for almost forty years.

After months of planning and saving up for an engagement ring, I finally mounted enough courage to pop the question to Juneall. Overthinking every proposal as too corny, I decided whenever the words were able to come out of my mouth, there would be no time like the present. By the end of the break, I tried to muster the words "Will you marry me?" on several occasions, but they wouldn't escape my mouth. Finally, by the weekend, I talked myself into "ripping it off like a Band-Aid"; otherwise, I'd never allow myself to say the words. The night while watching television, I turned down the volume and said I wanted to have a talk with Juneall. After an awkward pause and her saying, "Well, what did you want to talk about?" I blurted, "We should get married… I love you and believe you feel the same…what do you…," before I could finish his sentence, Juneall jumped out of her seat and wrapped her arms around me happily agreeing.

Without a doubt, I knew that was the best decision of my life. Kindred spirits, best friends, partners in crime, Juneall was his everything.

With the wedding planned for well over a year, it allowed us sufficient time to plan. I would like to say it was a joint venture in planning, but Juneall made the majority of decisions regarding the color scheme, theme, DJ, and food among other items that needed to be arranged. I didn't mind; I enjoyed the experience. Although many of the items had been checked off our list, we still couldn't decide on a venue. Each venue we checked out just didn't seem like a good fit. Finally, after months of searching, we picked an all-in-one venue that allowed for the wedding and post-reception to be held back to back, saving time and money. Another bonus was instead of paying for an open bar, both families were allowed to supply their own alcohol.

With the wedding all planned out, we followed through with their next international trip joking that it was our "pre-honeymoon." For our next expedition, we wanted to go farther than we had ever before. One of the main factors that lead us to agree on a destination was solely based on Juneall's love for ethnic food. Using her palate to guide the way to our next destination, we made plans to travel to Phuket, Thailand.

To supplement income and budget their travels, we began dog sitting through the online dog sitting company, Rover. The more clients and dogs they took in, the more experience they gained. After a few short months, the job had become second nature. Seeing many of the same dogs, they had the opportunity to build a connection with each dog and get to know their personalities. With a higher level of knowledge, we were able to categorize which dogs would and wouldn't get along as to ensure a safe environment. At one point in time, we would have up to six dogs at a time in our two-bedroom, one-bathroom duplex.

Over the next two years, we gradually saved our money toward traveling expenses and buying our first home.

It took a year and a half for us to save up enough funds, but we finally did. That summer, we hopped aboard a plane and after layovers in Hong Kong and Singapore arrived early in the morning to our tropical destination of Phuket.

Shortly before arriving, I looked out my window at the lushness of green contrasting with the pure aqua blue of the Pacific Ocean; it was absolutely magnificent. Upon arrival, we snagged the first taxi they could after getting our luggage. During the first few days, we stayed above an Irish pub that catered to Westerners; Juneall was in charge of booking the hotels and put together an opaque itinerary. She joked she wanted to stay above a pub so when I was craving for Guinness, it'd only be a short walk down a flight of stairs. She also joked, "So, you're going to be able to keep down your Guinness this trip!"

Settling into the hotel, Juneall took a shower and "freshened up," while I went downstairs to have my Guinness. Sitting on the patio sipping his beer, I observed a group of attractive young women conjured outside a massage parlor across the street. I knew prostitution was rampant in Thailand but had no idea the extent. After only a few seconds, two of the women approached asking if I would like to "boom-boom and party." Flattered, I thanked the prostitutes for the offer but said I was not interested. They blew me kisses and walked back across the street.

Juneall was behind me during the ordeal. Shortly after the two left, he heard Juneall's voice hysterically laughing, "Hahahahaha… I guess they sure know how to make a man feel welcome! What do you say? Let's give them business." We both couldn't stop laughing, and it seemed to take the edge off any anxiety she had been feeling.

We later gave the prostitutes business but not pertaining to sex; we both paid for massages every other day. A friendly bunch of women became our unofficial guides to help plan our activities and provided recommendations on where to eat, what parts of town to stay away from, and so on. Surely, we could have been recommending them to their cronies for their own benefit, but Juneall and I didn't care; every experience seemed to open our eyes.

Dogs adrift on the beach, tuk tuks around every corner, motorbikes, lady boys (transgendered individuals), crystal clear turquoise water, Buddhist temples, ferries, and speed boats all protrude in his memories of the trip. However, backtracking to the original reason we traveled to Thailand, we were in love with the food. Every dish seemed to flawlessly combine sweet, salty, sour, and spicy while emitting some of the heavenliest scents ever smelled.

For breakfast, lunch, and dinner, I tried every restaurants' Pad Thai. Unable to determine who took the title of "best Pad Thai in Phuket," I said it was too close to compare and called it a draw.

After several days in Phuket, Jenny and I hopped a ferry bound for the small island Ko Lanta located off the coast of Krabi. Unfortunately and unexpectedly, we didn't have the comfortable stay we were hoping for. In the first hotel we checked into, we appeared to be the only guests staying at the hotel; it was a complete ghost town other than the receptionist working at the front desk during work hours. Within seconds of checking out our room, we both spotted bugs crawling all over the bed, wall, and bathroom. We shook their heads in disbelief and immediately spoke to the lady at the front desk requesting another room. Another room was provided, but it too had bugs. Juneall didn't want to offend the hotel worker, but I wasn't so even keel. We decided to cut our losses and would take our luck with another hotel on the island.

The next hotel didn't have bugs so that was definitely a plus for us. It didn't have the amenities of a four- or five-star hotel, but it had an excellent pool and lounge area. Already enjoying their hotel better than their last option, we were also ready to again explore the nearby beach. However, the beach didn't look like it had in all the online pictures. Tons upon metric tons of rubbish was washed onto the beach with the tide. We came to find out how bad water pollution is in Southeast Asia. Many of the resorts hire individuals to clean the beach throughout the day to keep it clean. Since it wasn't tourist season, no one cleaned the beach (or so they were told by the receptionist at their hotel). "Oh well, at least there's no bugs in our room," I joked.

We made the most of our time and ended up having a blast. With no taxis or tuk tuks around, transportation by foot was like moving at a snail's pace. To explore, we rented a motorbike, and we set off exploring the island. Ko Lanta was far different from the touristy Phuket. The residents of Ko Lanta still thrived on tourism, but many of their people lived their lives every day as they had for decades. Farming and fishing thrived on the island, and there was a strong Islamic influence among its residents.

For their last leg of the trip, we stayed two nights in a five-star hotel located near the Phuket Airport. It was swanky, but after our experience in Ko Lanta, we were ready to bask in luxury. After our two-day stay in luxury, we took a taxi to the airport and waved good-bye as their plane took off.

With our first "really, really long trip" under our belts, we made plans for where our next trip would land us. Juneall and I considered numerous areas of the world but allowed fate to decide via a round-robin game of rock, paper, scissors. India ended up being "the winner," and a year and a half later, we were bound for South Asia.

However, there was still a year and a half before our next trip. We still had a wedding to throw. The days leading up to the wedding were surprisingly smooth. We weren't nervous; it was amusing everyone around seemed to be stressing out but us. Along with marrying the woman of my dreams, I was excited my mother would be able to make the trip.

Battling terminal cancer with a shortened prognosis, my mother's health was in a constant flux and was unsure if she would be healthy enough to make it to the wedding. When her health seemed to be waning with no improvement in sight, she did the miraculous; she forced herself to build up enough strength to go to the wedding. She told me, "I'm going to be there if it kills me...just you watch." Beginning with a lap around the house (with assistance from her walker) for her first few days of "training," she gradually increased the number of laps. After months of her own training regime, she had the strength to fly to the wedding.

I will never forget how nervous my mother was for the mother-son dance. She knew she couldn't stand on her own and didn't quite know what she was going to do. I comforted her and assured her he had a plan. With Whiney Houston's *Wind Beneath My Wings* playing, I helped my mother out of the wheelchair utilizing a full physical prompt. Once she was standing, I held onto her tight with an overhook and underhook supporting her from beneath her armpits. After the song was over, we continued to dance.

My mother made it a point to tell him she was so proud of me and this was one of the happiest days of her life.

Once the wedding weekend was finished, we began our new legally binding partnership. Working full-time and dog sitting part-time, the year flew by.

Entering my fourth and final year at the day treatment school, changes in organizational leadership brought major changes affecting the everyday teachers at the school. I wasn't so fortunate to have a constant assistant staff present in my classroom the last year at the school. With a change in organization policy, I was stuck with a revolving door or support staff which made the job even harder. Mentally, I was burning out and numerous times communicated that without the ability to take breaks, I was working a pace that couldn't be kept and couldn't properly cope with the stress of the job.

My friend, a therapist at the school, listened to me and provided a recommendation. She knew how challenging the job was and also could tell I was running out of ways to cope. Knowing the medical benefits of marijuana, she spoke to me about my feelings toward the topic. I always viewed pot with a stigma that had been embedded in my head from an early age. I never seriously considered using marijuana for its medical benefits until Abby had a serious talk with me. She believed it would help me but had no idea the impact the plant would have on my future.

Throughout my four years at the school, I had the reputation of being an excellent teacher but was unable to work with other staff; I drove away every paraprofessional making me the teacher no one wanted to work with. The director even communicated to me that many paraprofessionals refused to work with me, and it most definitely was a problem. Even at the age of thirty-three, I continued justifying the paraprofessionals were the problem and it wasn't me.

Once I began smoking marijuana, the days of driving away paraprofessionals seemed to be a thing of the past. Almost instantly, anger, anxiety, depression, and paranoia all seemed to fade. I could sit still when sitting with Juneall. I could maintain eye contact and actively listen to others throughout discourse. I felt and displayed greater levels of empathy for those around me. Physically, I could finally take a deep breath. A full night's rest was finally obtainable… no more sleepless nights perseverating over anything I could stress about.

My overall physical and emotional health greatly improved. Friends, colleagues, and supervisors all took notice and gave words of encouragement. My boss even sincerely told him, "You seem so much happier," and said I was the life of the party in the hallway before and after school when staff would conjure and chat it up.

I had smoked pot before but didn't like the way it made me feel. Understandably, this was usually after a hefty amount of drinking making me nauseous. I credited my partial rewiring to my marijuana usage when I was sober along with taking my prescribed low dose of Zoloft.

Arguably, one of the most influential jazz musicians of all time, Louis Armstrong, quoted marijuana, "It relaxes you, makes you forget all the bad things…" Chemically, I didn't know what was going on in my brain, but I loved it. I was finally feeling happy, and for the first time in years, my irrational fears seemed to fade.

With this new self-confidence and ability to cope with the stressors of life, I upped my professional game to an unparalleled level. I quickly came to be relied on as the most efficient teacher in the organization. The next few months, I was so settled into my job; it was as easy as riding a bike.

That winter, after another year and a half of saving, we were destined for Goa, India.

Arriving at the Goa International Airport, we stayed two nights in the airport's city of Vasco de Gamma. Juneall slept nearly the entire two days because of her jet lag; she didn't sleep well on the plane and was running on fumes. I waited for the sun to rise and set out exploring. Walking the streets of India opened my eyes to a whole new world of poverty never before seen. With some homes no more than tin shacks, I was heartbroken many peoples still live in such conditions.

After returning from my walk, I was hoping Juneall was awake so we could try and excercise. Jenny was out like a lamp and wouldn't budge. With no fitness center provided at the hotel, I flipped through the television channels and planned on doing sit-ups and push-ups while watching television. With all the channels provided, I flipped through until finding the Bollywood music video channel. I didn't know what the channel was called; I just referred to it as such. As foolish as I may have looked, I did my best to follow along with the beat and dance moves to every song. Every song seemed to be perfectly choreographed. After two songs, I was completely drenched in sweat. To this day, my favorite workout is dancing to Bollywood dance music.

After Juneall was rested, we took a taxi to their beach destination. Approximately an hour to reach our beach destination, our drive was terrifying. The first thing we noticed was the extreme difference in traffic laws. Thailand was similar but drew no comparison to the Indian experience. Passing cars going uphill, it was impossible to see oncoming traffic. Almost as if it were a game of chicken, both cars would keep the same speed, but oncoming cars would swerve off the road to avoid accidents. Juneall and I arrived in one piece and checked into our hotel upon arrival.

Just as we had in Thailand, we went out in search of the beach (which was much cleaner and rid of rubbish). Goa thrived on the tourist industry so the area provided endless options for entertainment. The "go-to" in Goa is to find your favorite beach shack on the beach, settle in, and spend the day eating, drinking, and relaxing. During the first full day on the beach, we rang up a total bill of just over US $35. Unlike Thailand, we didn't want to venture far from their hotel. We were looking to enjoy our immediate surroundings with as much fruition as possible.

Besides the beach vibe vacation, we incorporated meditation and yoga as much as possible. I used the time to make sense of myself and the world around me. Staying at a five-star resort, it was easy to appreciate how lucky we were when just outside the gates were some of the most extreme cases of poverty we had ever been exposed to. As cliché as it sounds, my experience left an everlasting impression and opened my mind. As Anthony Bourdain spoke of travel, "Travel is about the gorgeous feeling of teetering in the unknown."

Returning from India at the end of winter break, I was refreshed, rejuvenated, and ready to finish the remaining semester of work. Shortly after returning, Juneall and I welcomed our newest addition to our family, Carol the pitbull, Australian shepard mixed puppy. Rescued at ten weeks old, Carol had beautiful, smooth black fur that drooped off her body. Still growing into her humorously large puppy paws, she was awkward when she would run or walk. After looking into her eyes, we knew we had to have her. We both fell for her hard.

Juneall's dog Angus would now have a permanent sidekick. The training was symple as Carol followed the lead of Angus who was eight years old at the time. Also beneficial was exposing her to other trained dogs being dog sat. Within two short months, she was house trained.

THE WORST OF TIMES

By February, my mother was officially in remission, ringing the bell to signal the end of her grueling chemotherapy treatment; she was escorted out the building with her loving husband, my father, by her side. Beneath her Daffy Duck mask, she was smiling from ear to ear, and so was everyone in her life. Family and friends all celebrated the great news: she had beaten her prognosis and was considered a medical miracle in the health community.

The high would come to a screeching halt upon receiving the devastating news that unexpectedly, she passed after complications following a common cold that quickly escalated. Given the state of her body after intensive rounds of chemotherapy, her immune system was akin to that of a baby's. She was checked into the hospital for precautionary measures.

Checking on my mother throughout the week, I remember she had to text because she was too weak to talk. I naively thought everything was going to be fine and she would get better as she had always before. On that Thursday at 9:30, I received a call from my father. "Hey, Dad… What's up? How's Mom?" Silence. Silence quickly transitioned to muffled hysteria as my father tried his best to stay strong and deliver the news… Knowing something was seriously wrong, I again asked, "Dad, is she okay?" I didn't receive the news I was expecting, "Your mother passed a little bit ago… I don't know what I'm going to do! What am I going to do without her!"

With the funeral several weeks away, I returned home for approximately a month to help my father grieve during the "worst of times" and assist with making arrangements. Still in shock, my father was completely devastated. Losing his better half, he sank into a deep depression unable to accept or comprehend what had happened. One week, she was fine, and the next, she was gone. None of my family knew why it was her time to go, just that her time was up.

Catching the next flight home, I returned to my home town to provide my father and family support in any way I could. My boss was fully supportive and gave me the green light to "take as much time as needed with no questions asked." During his time back home, I didn't sleep much; I couldn't. A lifetime of memories replayed in my head like a movie, and I couldn't rest. To help out, I thoroughly cleaned my parents' house from top to bottom. I cleaned, cooked, and did anything I could to bring about even the slightest bit of light in such a dark time.

Returning to work after a month, I was openly consoled and met with support from my colleagues. Excited to get back to work and begin a routine that would help me grieve with his loss, I would wake up early to clean beginning at 4 a.m. and tidy up until reporting to work at 7:30 a.m. Returning home after an eight-hour workday, I would again clean till approximately 1 a.m., take a power nap, and begin the cycle all over again. As expected, my weight drastically plummeted like the stock market following the emergence of COVID-19.

I had shed nearly thirty pounds and physically looked gaunt and frail. Staff repeatedly checked on my well-being, but every time, I would ensure everyone I was fine and would paste a smile on his face. Everyone could see I wasn't doing well but myself. I was a duck—calm and collected on the exterior but violently flailing underneath the surface. I continued working this pace until the end of the school year fully intending on returning the next academic school year, but plans wouldn't go accordingly.

The last week before Memorial Day weekend, Juneall's parents urged me to quit my job, for my mental well-being and sanity.

I couldn't shake the feelings I was garnering toward his students. My classroom was a hostile environment that Friday.

The compounding of lifelong angst spilled while sitting at my teacher's desk. The chronic ache of burnout had come to a boiling point, and I couldn't take it anymore. Sensing distress, some of the students jumped on the opportunity to "kick a man while he's down" candidly bragging they were going to take bets to see who could make me "lose his shit."

Along with personally being in crisis, it infuriated me that the students whom I had built rapport with were so ready to "turn on me." I interpreted these words and actions as threats. I didn't care if the students had trauma or were fueled by their developmental selves to have the intrinsic desire to "fit in"; I felt I was being attacked with malice intentions given the obvious state I was in.

Practicing emotional intelligence, I radioed to staff I immediately needed a break...crickets. After calling another time, I got a response that no staff were available at that moment to relieve me. That was the last straw...underfunded; the school didn't have the manpower to keep the environment safe. Anytime I would leave the classroom, students would immediately take advantage of the lack of physical presence (almost always a male when working with the older students) to intervene if necessary.

As predicted, a near riot broke out when I left the classroom until other classrooms had to pull their resources to help. I wasn't selfish; I was a team player that had sacrificed so much for my students. After everything I had done for these kids, this is how they repaid me... At that moment, I didn't care if they had a trauma of their own. I just kept thinking in my head, "What about my fucking trauma?" I didn't return back to school; I knew I wouldn't be able to handle my emotions.

That night, I sat on his porch thinking about why I was so distraught. I had been able to find ways of coping before, but this time was different. I couldn't just move on.

The night before reporting back to work, I sat on his patio and let out a deep cry that echoed from my inside. This was the first time I had cried in years. I knew it was my time to "ride off into the sunset" from work, but I was conflicted. I was finally openly accepted and respected by my colleagues. Ninety-nine percent of the time I loved the job. The problem was the other 1%: riots, being spat on, bit, kicked, pinched, punched, slapped, and threatened professionally and personally... Vicarious trauma was eating away at my mental health. More than anything, I was scared of leaving knowing my choppy work history could "come back to haunt me." I knew what I had to do: I had to leave my job.

That Monday, I informed both bosses I would not be coming back. Both knew I had issues but not the severity of the extent. I informed them "I had lost his ability to cope" and was "going to beat the shit out of one of these kids if I worked one more day at the school." I wasn't a monster; I was a human advocating for myself and practicing emotional intelligence. After a few short minutes, the meeting had to be called short due to crises in the building unfolding at that moment.

After the meeting, I felt so relieved and proud of myself I finally had the strength and courage to leave my toxic work behind.

Later in the evening, both bosses stopped by my house to check in on me. Sitting on the back porch drinking whiskey and smoking a blunt, I heard a car door close in the driveway. My bosses were concerned and wanted to make sure I wasn't thinking about hurting myself or others. They informed me I did the right thing and that they knew something was seriously wrong. They informed me they were allowing me to finish the remaining week with a medical leave with full pay and stellar recommendations. I was and continue to remain close with both supervisors and am thankful they chose to stop by and check in on me.

You Quit Your Job? What Are You Going to Do Next?

After having the courage to "take a leap of faith" not knowing what the next steps would bring, I focused on securing a future teaching gig like I had had to do so many times before. However, this experience was different. I wasn't being pushed out; I had a village of support. I was betting on myself; basing my credentials and valuable work experience would easily land me my next teaching gig. I began scouring for every teaching position I qualified for.

At first, I immediately generated interest from numerous higher-paying, suburban "big league" districts. I was given a recommendation for hire by two of the districts, but both offers were eventually reneged. Just as I worried, my checkered past was sending a red flag to HR departments around the area. After the districts withdrew their original offers, I finally lost my shit and became psychotic: mentally, emotionally, and physically.

I knew I wasn't okay but was unprepared for my breaking point. My demeanor and personality changed erratically every other minute. One second, I'd be weeping uncontrollably stricken with anxiety; the next, I'd "snap out of it" instantly self-soothing with deep breathing only again shift into violent rage. Numerous tables and chairs were thrown around the house, and desks were tipped on their sides.

My wife and her parents procured me a therapy appointment as soon as possible. Showing up to the appointment, I wasn't okay. On the inside, I was nothing short of crazy, but somehow, I was able to keep the mask on I had used throughout my life with a remarkably calm demeanor. Even in one of the most vulnerable times in my life, I wouldn't allow myself to show how I was feeling on the inside.

Sitting on the therapy couch, the therapist and I smiled at one another. She soon asked in the typical soothing soft voice of a therapist, "So, what brings you in today?" I looked in her eyes, kept my calm demeanor, and calmly told her, "I'm not okay... I'm in crisis and need help... I'm afraid I may do something that will hurt someone or something." Her eyes widened and without hesitation stated, "We need to get you help...like right now." Directions were given to my wife, and she drove me to the nearest mental health facility.

As I walked into the facility, my mask followed. After handing over his belt, shoelaces, and personal items, I was escorted to a room by a burly man who appeared to be the "muscle" in case of instances of physical aggression. A therapist eventually came to the room and began asking questions evaluating if I was at risk of hurting myself or others. Surprisingly, I was discharged with the nurses recommending I return a few days later for a follow-up appointment to see another therapist prior to seeing the psychiatrist to be prescribed meds.

I wouldn't be able to make it to the following appointment.

The next day, I knew I couldn't go on with how I was feeling. I wasn't going to kill myself; I couldn't go on with the intensity and chronic shock I knew awaited my mind and body. I hysterically cried out to my wife to help, and without hesitation, she drove me back to the mental health facility.

After a lengthy day of seeing two therapists and a psychiatrist, I was diagnosed with PTSD and bipolar I disorder and prescribed the appropriate meds. Meds helped my mood which slowly stabilized over time. With weeks until the start of my new job in yet another school district, I did my best to mentally recharge.

Rest, Relaxation, and Miracle Gro

With a few short weeks until the next school year was to begin, my mind was still frazzled and felt the effects of burnout. Still struggling with the cognitive ability to complete minute tasks such as reading and writing, I joked with my therapist that I would try to get by on my good looks. On the recommendation of my therapist,

I immersed myself in caring for and maintaining our lawn and planting several gardens.

The goal was simple: to reconnect with nature in any way I could and provide a self-driven form of nature therapy. Tilling, aerating, seeding, watering, and pruning most wouldn't consider being strenuous exercise. I'd work from sunrise to sunset making sure to "work off" much of my stress.

Once work started up again, I would rush home to work outside until the sun was set. Still grieving the loss of my mother and acclimating to yet another job, working outdoors seemed to help clear my mind and helped my mood stay even keel. As I improved overall, so did my clarity. Transitioning from working solely for physical and emotional benefits that came with manual labor, I gradually began developing an appreciation for aesthetics. Working the land, I was always mindful of beauty and balance. The more aesthetically pleasing to the eye, the greater sense of pride I took. My mind was making leaps and bounds in my recovery.

My mood continued improving as my body gradually acclimated to the cocktail of meds prescribed. I still struggled with concentration but was in the process of being prescribed Adderall. The first few prescriptions were extremely low as to monitor my heart and ensure other psychiatric conditions weren't triggered. As the doses increased, I quickly began to notice life in a "before and after" lens.

As if Louis Armstrong's *What a Wonderful World* was the theme song to my life, I saw the world in color for the first time. Colors seemed crispier and brighter as if the fog glued to my headlights magically vanished. I finally had the ability to truly observe the world around me and objectively analyze my past. If I could make sense of my past and present, I can learn from my mistakes and continue growing emotionally, mentally, and spiritually.

With this growth and sense of self-realization, I possessed the ability and drive to once again strive for and reach my goals. My first goal was met with relative ease; I sought to manage my emotions, give my best effort, and be rewarded with a contract renewal for the following year. After receiving my contract for the following year, the world was soon ravished by the COVID-19 pandemic.

With my contract secured, I set his sights on bigger goals, generate more income, and continue to push myself to get out of his comfort zone.

COVID-19: PLENTY OF TIME TO THINK

After examining my past, I recognize who I am, what I like, and what "makes me tick."

Good and bad, I view every occurrence as a learning opportunity. I credit much of my development to my four years at the trauma-sensitive day treatment school. I gained valuable experience and knowledge, particularly in regard to utilizing coping strategies. I embraced the philosophy, "We respect ourselves, we respect others, and we respect our environment." These three simple rules are used on a daily basis to fruition. Although I used these primarily in the classroom, I came to the realization that logically, the strategies could be used in my personal life to better complete me.

"We respect ourselves" can be interpreted in many ways. I believe one of the initial steps to respecting myself is to be mindful of self-talk and the stewing of negativity swirling in my brain. When I'm feeling the darkness creeping into my mind, I take a step back and identify how I am feeling and why I feel that way. Catching myself in the act of being negative is effective at communicating I'm not in a good space and my self-talk needs to be adjusted accordingly.

Along with respecting my emotional health, I care for my physical health—brushing my teeth twice a day, ensuring I take my medications, indulging in vices with moderation, showering, etc. The concept is simple: since physical and emotional health are correlated to one another, the betterment of one area positively affects the other. I can be dressed to impress and physically look like Fabio in his prime, but if I'm in a negative headspace, my overall health will begin to deter.

"We respect our environment" is just as important to my over-all well-being. The secular interpretation of "cleanliness is godliness" speaks to the benefits of caring for yourself and the environment around you. Keeping the environment clean, organized, and tidy helps decrease my frustration, produces clearer thinking, and allows me to portray to others, "I'm doing pretty well, and I treat myself accordingly." Coincided, if I'm in an environment that is messy and unkempt, my anxiety waxes.

The major area of self-care I struggled with was advocating for myself in an assertive, nonaggressive way. Sadly, it's humbling for me to admit I've been taken advantage of and persuaded to do things against my better judgment. The bummer of having a low sense of self and pattern of allowing others to treat me poorly wasn't respecting myself.

Respecting others is exactly what it sounds like, the Golden Rule. Treat others the way one would like to be treated. Most don't appreciate being treated poorly or manipulated, so common sense suggests one ought not to treat others that way.

Matt, How Have You Been? It's Been Awhile

Bottom of the ninth, down by three, bases loaded, full count, two outs, no fear? The pitch was thrown, and twelve-year-old me watched as the ball crossed the plate without swinging. My coach was furious, and for good reason, if you don't swing the bat, you have a zero-percent chance of hitting the ball.

Much like in life, if one doesn't try to reach their goals, they'll never achieve them. In my case, my mental health has been the ball and chain shackled to my ankle, the weighted vest slowing my movement up the personal mountain of success. What has happened when I am finally able to shake adversity? No pun intended, but short answer—the possibilities are limitless.

The extra time allotted throughout the new normal has encouraged me to get out of my comfort zone and explore other avenues for generating income to live my life.

So…what am I doing to work toward my goal of financial security? I'm taking an approach to spend less and make more money.

Initially, I applied and was accepted into the administration master's program offered at one of the local universities. With several years to complete the program, I'm in no rush. Being enrolled in such a program opens windows of opportunities for me to continue down the path of education if I choose to do so. However, I ask myself, "Is the juice worth the squeeze?" I already owe plenty of money for my education; is adding more debt an investment that would lead to a higher salary worth it? Could be…but such a process can be lengthy and given my spotty work history, I may not be able to fully capitalize on my investment.

Stocks? The mentioning of the word was enough to cause anxiety. Visions of losing everything if you invest where the only scenarios Matt 1.0 would allow myself to picture. Currently, Matt 2.0 is using his noggin to self-educate and use my skills of reading data and recognizing psychological and social patterns to earn additional income through day trading on the stock market. My portfolio is diverse ensuring I don't put all my eggs in one basket. I'm making smart decisions and aiming to build up my "nest egg" in case I needs it (understanding the tax implications of when money is eventually taken out of my account). Being mindful of calculated exit strategies for each investment, I'm feeling confident.

Modeling? I never fancied myself a handsome fella, but a lifetime of people telling me, "You are really attractive... Do you ever think about modeling?" has finally started to sink in. I'm not Fabio in his prime or Missouri's own Brad Pitt; I'm me. I have confidence, swagger, and flavor which only accentuate my attractiveness. I'm not looking for full-time work, just spending money on the side for any gigs I land. Recently, submitting my cover shots to agencies, I figure why the hell not. Worst-case scenario, they're not interested... Oh well, at least, I put myself out there.

Acting? A skill set I have acquired through a lifetime of angst could potentially earn me additional money. Three decades of wearing a mask portraying what I wanted the outside world to see has allowed me to hone my acting skills. My previous life of bouncing from one identity to the next has given me the skill set to master the chameleon effect. Given a variety of scenarios, situations, and peoples, I am able to adapt and blend. As they say in the industry, "Fake it till you make it." Who knows, maybe one day, you as the reader will have the privilege of seeing my skills. Only time will tell, but again, if the industry isn't interested... Oh well, at least I put myself out there.

Writing? Ah, yes...writing. my new passion in life. Better than any drug I've been on, writing allows me to express myself unlike any other vessel has before. With the computer as my pedestal, my emotions escape from my heart, to my fingers, to the computer. My writing began as a form of self-therapy. One page quickly morphed to ten, ten turned into fifty, and so on. I am inspired to compose a novel and have it published. Still working on my own personal masterpiece, I have been in contact with an array of literary agents and publishing companies. I'm taking the steps needed to make my dream a reality, but again,…if the industry isn't interested…oh well, at least, I put myself out there.

Networking? Absolutely. Networking itself doesn't raise your income but provides opportunities that in return correlate into more income. Struggling with PTSD, I isolated myself for years from family and friends. I didn't care if I was a social hermit, as the Goo Goo Dolls proclaim, "And I don't want the world to see me, 'cause I don't think that they'd understand…" I am still in the process of reaching out to old friends, colleagues, and family members I haven't spoken to in years and have been met with mixed results. I've had to accept some may not want to keep in contact; I can't control their actions or how they feel. However, I've been met with open arms and acceptance from the majority of those I've reached out to.

Before acknowledging and accepting help, I wasn't able to take care of myself. If I couldn't help myself, logically, no way I could help others with validity. Like a superhero going through unforeseen circumstances only to emerge with powers, my metamorphosis allowed me to emerge with the skills needed to fulfill my desire to help others in any way I can.

Strong communication skills, confidence, charisma, patience, knowing when and how to show empathy, and displaying genuine interest in others are all these I consider personal strengths. Humans being social creatures, whether consciously or subconsciously, gravitate toward success; people are beginning to gravitate toward me.

With this new phenomenon, I realize I possess the ability to influence and inspire others. Mirroring my philosophy of education, you never know who you'll impact with those drops of influence. As the drops spread, the ripples become greater and greater. With pure virtue influence, those ripples have the potential to spread farther than ever imagined.

As I continue to grow, so too will my appreciation of every second, minute, and hour alive in this wonderful world. I love life and appreciate my good fortunes.

If you are reading these words, believe my work will continue... my three and a half decades of journey is far from over.

ABOUT THE AUTHOR

After graduating summa cum laude with highest honors in a degree of social studies education, Matthew J. Miller received his master›s degree in special education. From the onset of his teaching career, his mental health remained undiagnosed and untreated resulting in repeated jobs being lost.

Eight years into his teaching career as a special education teacher, he experienced a mental breakdown and was subsequently diagnosed with PTSD, bipolar I, ADHD, and generalized anxiety disorder. After a year of intense rewiring (due to "heavy duty" meds and therapy), he's discovered his true purpose in life, helping others. He began writing as a form of therapy and soon discovered his inner catharsis. In a month's time, he composed his first book *Manic, Anxious, and the Pursuit of Meds* and has plans on future literary endeavors.